HOW TO TAKE THE HEADACHE OUT OF CONTENT RESEARCH

TOP 9 QUESTIONS ANSWERED

By

C.S. ZAHN

"Content: there is no easy button." ~ Scott Abel, Content Strategist

INTRODUCTION

I think that the quote that I placed on the preceding page is a good start for this book on content research. Finding good content for an article, eBook, or podcast is not easy. There is a lot of information available on the World Wide Web. Some good, some not so good. Weeding through it all can be a very daunting task.

As an online marketer, your business needs a decent content strategy. In order to create acceptable content, you need to know how and where to find it. This will demand extensive research on your part.

It is my intent, through this book, to give you various tools that you can use to make researching your next subject matter easier.

Table of Contents

CHAPTER 1. WHY DOES GOOD RESEARCH MATTER?

Good research matters for many reasons. Gone are the good old days of keyword stuffing to rank on page one of Google and other search engines. Today it takes a little more effort to make money from a product, service or website, but it is more than worth it. If you want to promote a standing as the ultimate authority in any niche or market and grow an ardent following, simply using a keyword over and over does not get the job done. You, without question, must produce considerable amounts of actionable and first-rate information which is both easy to understand and relevant to your market.

Think about your own experiences when searching for answers on the World Wide Web. Isn't it annoying when you land on a squeeze page, click on an advertisement, follow a Facebook post or Twitter tweet only to find yourself on a website with very little and/or poor information? Even if that specific website owner were to become the premier expert in his or her field, you still may never go back.

The old adage that "you never get a second chance to make a first impression" is even more significant online, where very small attention spans and demanding web surfers just will not put up with a poorly researched piece of content.

Research helps you to be a real authority

Besides the noticeable benefits that your social media followers or list members receive, concentrated and wide-ranging research helps you as well. Just by carrying out more research than your competition, you are automatically and subconsciously becoming more and more self-confident when speaking or writing about your specific market, product or service.

Whether you are conveying your information through video, audio or text, your level of confidence and expertise will directly relate to how you are received by those who see your content online.

Taking time to properly research content you are publishing online also puts you in the practice of doing more for your followers, readers and video viewers than the bare minimum.

You will begin to assuredly feel like an authority, while at the same time you are seen as a leading expert in your market. The law of reciprocity will compensate you in the future for the hard work and thorough research you perform before releasing it to your audience.

As you can see, doing good research is a win-win situation. You become a real authority, and help others as a result.

Now it's time to learn more about exactly how to do that research.

CHAPTER 2. HOW DOES "NICHING DOWN" YOUR MARKET MAKE RESEARCH EASIER?

You know that research matters, for many reasons. But almost every market, both online and offline, can have numerous parts that need to be properly researched.

Make your research easier

This is the main reason you need to know your market. When you know exactly what your prospective customers are really looking for, you can then focus in and deliver those very exact needs.

Quickly become an authority in your niche

The second advantage of narrowing your emphasis during the research phase of content creation is speed. Since you are spending less time researching a huge marketplace, you become an authority in a smaller niche much more quickly. This gives you more time to work on product development.

Now that you have narrowed down your focus, how do you find out what questions they are asking? If you want to discover those questions that are burning in the minds of your prospective customers, you need to go to places online where they are asking for help in clearing the smoke out of their lives. Then your research efforts will be a piece of cake.

CHAPTER 3. WHERE CAN I GO TO FIND THE QUESTIONS THAT MY COMMUNITY WANTS ANSWERED?

The Internet is a very social place. We will explore how social media can help you create excellent content later on in this guide. But Facebook and Twitter are not the only places you need to be frequenting if you want to know the burning questions your market is asking.

Forums in you niche

You can use the power of Google to know just what the marketplace is looking for. Type "your niche + forums" into Google to find forums in your niche. Some require that you sign up with an email address. When you do this, you will be on their mailing list and receive updates on things going on within the forum. Forums can provide you with some free inside information to help you create relevant and timely content for your market.

For instance, if your market is sunflower gardeners, you would type "sunflower gardening forums" into

Google for a list of relevant hangouts where gardeners discuss that topic. Forums are an excellent place to find those questions that your community wants answered.

An additional benefit when you join a forum central to your niche is that you can answer other member's questions. Once you start answering questions and solving other member's problems, you will start branding yourself as an authority figure.

And by placing a link back to your website or blog in the signature file you create when you join a forum, you develop not only powerful and industry relevant backlinks, but also free traffic.

Yahoo answers

Yahoo Answers, answers.yahoo.com, is also an excellent resource that you can use for quality content creation. Picture a central site where web surfers in your market congregate, asking questions that trouble them the most.

The questions you will find in Yahoo Answers are total diamonds to a marketer such as you. Those single questions can be used to form chapters for an eBook, slides in a slideshow presentation, a YouTube video, or an awesome blog post.

Registering for a free account at Yahoo Answers allows you to answer those questions that people in your market are asking, further building your brand.

Ask.com

The Ask.com home page is streamlined, and simple. Ask.com's search technology responds to questions, phrases, or single word searches. In addition to the standard Web search, you can also search for images, news, maps, local search, weather, encyclopedia listings, blogs and feeds, and more.

Using Amazon products for your research

Another exceptional way to research great topics for your content creation is to go to Amazon. Search for the bestselling books in your niche, and then click on each one of them in turn.

Amazon lets you view the table of contents for any book you choose. Take the chapter titles from the bestselling books in your niche, reword them, and use them to successfully write your own "bestselling" content.

Note: This does not mean copying the book in any way. Chapters should be used for general ideas. You can then dig deeper and find related subtopics to use as content titles and article ideas, rather than taking any information from the main text itself.

CHAPTER 4. HOW DO I FIND RELIABLE SOURCES ABOUT FACTS & FIGURES?

You have collected some really great questions that you know your market wants answers to. So how do you get reliable facts and figures online to solve the problems of people in your niche?

Numbers are powerful, and they can help to establish you as an authority figure in your niche. But you have to make certain that the statistics and data you are using are totally correct.

How Reliable is Google?

One very common way to obtain statistical information and other pertinent data is to use Google.

We are not talking about searching for a fact and using the first answer Google gives you. That is not the way to do reliable research. How do you know that source is correct?

Instead, we're using Google to find further sources of reliable information.

Other useful sources for facts you can rely on

Since you always want to double and triple check your information, there are some excellent spots online where you can be sure your research will produce reliable numbers and data.

Do you need to know US demographics? Head over to **Census.gov.** That is the official Census Bureau for the United States government. The website has a specific area titled Research, where tons of free and accurate geographical, personal and business data can be found.

Are you in a medical market? Then you will want to head over to **MedlinePlus.gov** to access medical research that has been conducted and published by the United States National Library of Medicine.

Statistics.gov.uk handles official United Kingdom statistics in a wide variety of areas, and is the National Statistics headquarters of the UK.

Abs.Gov.au is the Australian equivalent, where you can research facts and figures compiled by the Australian Bureau of Statistics.

A very powerful tool that lets you know exactly how web surfers access information and consume it can be found at **us.Nielsen.com**. This versatile website also shows you how and why consumers buy goods and services.

Looking for a virtual library? A **Questia.com** membership provides access to over 1.5 million books in print on a variety of subjects.

And the self-explanatory **FactCheck.org** will help you research claims, facts and figures made during political campaigns, including but not limited to taxes and healthcare.

These few resources for research are the proverbial tip of the online iceberg when it comes to reliable web locations for verifiable statistics and data.

Simply type into Google "statistics about + your niche" to get a list of excellent sources for information on your market, and as you dig for data, take note of recurring keywords which you can use later.

CHAPTER 5. HOW DO I USE KEYWORD RESEARCH FOR CONTENT IDEAS?

Now that you know what questions to ask and where to find dependable and provable data, you need to make the search engines and your prospective customers satisfied. That means filling your content with keywords, phrases and relevant themed information that is market-specific.

Google Keyword Planner

Google has retired their old keyword tool, retooled it and renamed it Keyword Planner.

You may see a recurring theme in this online research guide regarding Google. There is a very good reason for that. Google controls more than two thirds of the online search market place, and they have compiled many terabytes of data. Why not let them do the hard keyword researching work?

Log into your Google account on the AdWords page, and then click on Tools and Analysis > Keyword

Planner. Then click on Search for keyword ideas. If you do not have a Google or Gmail account, setting one up is quick and easy, and gives you access to this wonderful and free keyword research tool.

This allows you to search keywords for content ideas according to products and services, the landing page on your website or blog, and your product category or niche. Clicking the "Get Ideas" button and then "Keyword Ideas" after the results populate will give you a wealth of relevant information.

Bing Keyword Research

The Bing search engine can help you with your keyword research as well, and if you head over to the Bing Keyword Research page and sign-up for a Bing Webmasters account, you have free access to all the keywords, phrases and themes that Bing finds relevant to your niche.

Bing and Google can also provide excellent insight about your website concerning SEO and traffic as a bonus.

Other free keyword tools

Some other great and free keyword research tools are:

Word tracker – http://www.wordtracker.com/

A popular and well-known piece of online keyword research equipment, Wordtracker boasts a very easy to use interface and speedy results. It actually lets you know exactly what people are searching for on the World Wide Web. They are currently offering a no risk 7-day free trial. After that pricing starts at $27.00 USD per month.

WordStream Keyword Tool –
http://www.wordstream.com/keywords

 This tool allows you to perform custom-made searches of a huge database with several filtering levels. You can also identify negative keywords and other niches which relate to your relevant keywords and phrases. The keyword tool is free.

SEO Book Keyword Tool -

http://tools.seobook.com/keyword-tools/

SEO Book is an outstanding keyword research tool that is also free. It actually sorts by volume for all the top search engines. SEO Book Keyword Tool will break down search numbers by market share for Google, Yahoo, and Bing, so you can see which keywords relevant to your market appear across all the major search engines. They offer both free and paid services.

CHAPTER 6. HOW DO I USE CURRENT EVENTS TO DESCRIBE MY RESEARCH?

Using free keyword research tools online for content ideas is an easy and smart tactic for developing pertinent content-based products. However, sometimes you may want to piggyback on hot trends or new product releases. This is also an excellent way to get free and massive traffic, and can make online content research a snap.

Many keyword tools are free and powerful, as well as easy to use but they won't tell you hot new trends. But did you know that Google has a free piece of software that works per your commands 24/7?

Google Alerts

You can actually tell Google what information you want according to your chosen keywords and phrases. Then the Google Alerts system will let you know the instant that any news or data which falls under your search criteria hits the World Wide Web.

This is not only an incredible way to put the world's largest search engine to work for you during your content research efforts, it is also an exceptional way to find out what hot trends and breaking news are hitting your market. You can be alerted to new product releases, become an affiliate for that company, send an e-mail to your list or make a blog post within minutes of the product launch.

This places you at the head of your industry, and can also disclose some great information, data and current events which will assist you in creating news-like content that sets you as a market leader.

Head over to http://www.google.com/alerts, type in a search query and choose all results or filter by books, news, blogs and other formats. Set up the regularity with which you would like the results delivered, and enter your e-mail address.

It is as easy as that to put a multibillion-dollar data chomping company to work for you, doing much of your online content research.

Google Trends

Google Trends is located at http://www.google.com/trends, and this great free tool that gives you real-time access to the hottest searches and trends which are happening right now. You can also search niche keywords and phrases, and other topics important to your market. Cyclical information allows you to look back over time to see exactly when a specific search term or keyword is most popular.

Google Trends and Alerts are very authoritative and productive tools every online researcher should be using. And the last few years, social media and networking sites have exploded as a way to find out what's hot and what's important to your community.

CHAPTER 7. HOW DO I USE SOCIAL MEDIA AS A RESEARCH TOOL?

Did you know that websites like Facebook and Twitter have built-in market research tools you can use for free? If you are concentrating on content delivery to any online social network, use the marketing tools that each particular site offers.

Facebook

Facebook currently boasts more than one billion users. That is more than one seventh of the world's population. And while Mark Zuckerberg and his team of engineers and developers can sometimes frustrate online marketers with their constantly changing advertising system, they do have some excellent research tools built right into the world's largest and most popular online social network.

When a billion-dollar company has one billion users continuously entering search data and other requests on its website, they group that information and use it in their marketing efforts. And now you can access much of that data for free.

A great way to use Facebook as a research tool is to build a fan page and begin asking your fans questions that get them involved.

Remember, this is a social network, not a retail store. Facebook should be about delivering content, information, videos and pictures that pluck the emotional heartstrings of your market. Build a market relevant fan page with lots of great information that you have obtained using the previous steps we talk about in this guide, and then ask your fans exactly what they are looking for.

Option 2 – follow other fan pages

The information you receive on a social networking platform like Facebook is truly what people want and desire.

You should also start following other pages in your niche, even though these are your competitors. Lurk on their fan pages and see what people in your market are talking about and sharing. This is valuable and free online content research.

Option 3 – graph search

You can complement your Facebook research even further using the new Graph Search feature. A tutorial for Facebook's marvelous new site searching tool can be found at https://www.facebook.com/about/graphsearch.

Can you begin to see the power of the Facebook Graph Search?

Option 4 – hashtags

Facebook has also unabashedly copycatted a Twitter tool, and has its own hashtag version. By typing #sunflower or #sunflowers into the Facebook search bar, you are delivered to every single instance where someone posted that very hashtag.

This can give you access to the Facebook users interested in your topic or market, as well as give you pertinent research on just what your competition is doing on the world's largest social networking website.

But since Facebook is not the only social media hangout online, you should also explore content research at Twitter, Pinterest and the other top sharing-based Internet social networks.

Pinterest and Twitter can both provide excellent research opportunities, so let's take a look at these two major social media players.

Pinterest

As of 2013, 21% of all online adults located in the United States used Pinterest (70 million). With four times as many female as male users, Pinterest is a treasure trove of female demographic information. Mostly users between 18 and 49 years of age, the typical Pinterest pinner builds Boards which they then give a topic name or description.

They Pin pictures, videos, infographics and other information on their boards that they find useful, fun or worthy of sharing with others interested in the same niche.

Just know that using Pinterest as a research tool requires time. You have to do the work. But by looking through the boards and pins of other Pinterest users in your niche, you can find images, recipes, products, keywords and phrases that are pertinent to your field.

And when you type a word or phrase into the Pinterest search field, you have access to all the users and pins relevant to that topic.

Twitter

Through January of 2014, a full 18% of all Internet users were tweeting away on Twitter. Nearly a third of all Twitter users are 18 to 29, and most of them are accessing this quick moving social network from their mobile phone.

There are many ways to put the power of Twitter to work for you, but easily the most powerful and easy-to-use research tool on that network is the hashtag. The precursor to the Facebook hashtag, Twitter's version works the same way.

First, head over to the Twitter search page and log into your account. (*Tip* Remember that you can have a Twitter account and design developed for just $5 at Fiverr.com.)

Then type into the Twitter search box the # symbol, followed by whatever phrase, keyword or term you want to research. In just a few seconds, you will see a list of the most recent tweets that contain that hashtag and phrase.

Many users on Twitter link to news items, products, videos and other content when they use a hashtag. This can reveal different types of media and information that would be perfect for your eBook, blog post, list of e-mail subscribers or Facebook followers.

Researching in our example niche, #sunflowers on Twitter shows that you can narrow your search by photos, news or video, or simply browse tweets where that hashtag was used.

Now that you have learned some powerful and free online tools and tips that can help you speedily conduct research for your content creation projects, it's time to get organized.

CHAPTER 8. HOW DO I ORGANIZE MY RESEARCH?

You might wonder why a section on organizing your research is necessary. However, once you delve deeper into creating content for your niche, you're going to find that you come up with ideas and new research sources quicker than you can keep up with them. This is why it's crucial to stay organized.

If you can efficiently research and organize your information, you can establish and maintain a position as an authority figure in your marketplace. And the wonderful technologies available to the online marketer today make organizing your research simple, speedy and available anywhere there is a stable Internet connection.

Many of the popular applications that marketers use to stay organized online like Evernote and Scrivener offer true mobile access from virtually any location, for your smartphone, mobile PC or tablet, or the nearest desktop computer.

Evernote

Download page: https://evernote.com/evernote/

Evernote's tag line is that the company "makes it easy to remember things big and small from your everyday life using your computer, phone, tablet and the web." And that is really how the company works.

Free downloads are offered for both Mac and PC, and multiple mobile operating systems like Android and iOS. You can then download data, information and media into your Evernote account from any device with an Internet connection.

Imagine a virtual filing cabinet that you can access any time day or night, from any of your Web powered devices, and you can see how this wonderful free application can help you organize your research effectively.

Workflowy

Download page: https://workflowy.com/

Workflowy is a great piece of software for compiling to-do lists and managing your tasks. The company says it can help you "organize your brain", and this note-taking application offers the anywhere, all-time access that is central to accessing and organizing your research no matter when or where the mood strikes you.

Scrivener

Download page:
http://literatureandlatte.com/scrivener.php

Scrivener is an effective piece of word processing software that also acts as a management system for organizing notes and documents. Support for text, PDF, audio, video and images is present, and this is a very popular content organization tool for authors.

You can conveniently drag and drop customized virtual index cards onto your cyber corkboard, and employ a split-screen mode which enables you to multitask, editing several documents at once.

Instapaper

Download page: http://www.instapaper.com/

Instapaper is another free application which allows you to turn web content, including blog posts, e-mails, articles and videos, into a text-based reading experience. This browser-based application requires no download, and allows you to simply save content that you see throughout your busy day for access later.

You just click a button in your browser on your PC, or choose "send to Instapaper" on your mobile computer or smartphone. A big part of the popularity here is the extremely simple and uncluttered user interface.

Typing "top tools for getting organized online" into Google or any other search engine will allow you to browse the most effective and popular research and content organizing tools, both free and paid, that the web has to offer.

The key is finding a tool that works for you. And, yes, it will take time to get used to using a tool and finding a system, but once it's done you'll save hours.

CHAPTER 9. HOW DO I LEARN FROM THE COMPETITION?

Researching content online reveals that there are plentiful ways to find information and media that is relevant to your niche. But one of the best ways to find out just what type of content you should be creating and delivering is to become a private investigator!

Your competitors are a treasure trove of market-relative information. So why don't you let them do all the hard work and market research?

Email newsletters

One great way to harness the research efforts of one of your competitors is to sign up as an e-mail subscriber on their website.

Go to your Gmail or e-mail account, and set up a separate folder with the name of the competitor that you just subscribed to. As you begin to receive auto responder e-mail messages from your fellow marketer, stick them in that folder.

Break down the e-mails when you receive them, read them several times, and think like a potential customer. When you get e-mails from a competitor that are compelling and that actually make you want to take the requested action, you can format and word your own e-mails in a similar fashion when delivering content to your marketplace.

Websites

You can also visually examine and investigate the top websites of your competition. It would be foolish to exactly replicate the theme and look of one of your competitor's websites. And you never want to exactly copy any e-mails or other content that they are delivering.

But by watching how they use breaking news to tie into relevant market content, you can develop your own successful systems and strategies. Also, if you find that a particular website in your market or field seems to have substantial comments on blog posts, that social interaction is absolutely invaluable. How did that website owner engage readers to get them to comment? Did they directly ask for comments and ideas? Or maybe they included a lot of videos and infographics which got their readers thinking, and feeling emotions, which then drove them to feel the need to comment.

There is no need to reinvent the wheel when you find a strategy that is successfully being used by your competitors. Simply tweak whatever they are doing for your unique style, and begin delivering online content in that way.

Social media spying

A few more simple ways to ethically "spy" on your competitors is to join their Facebook fan pages, follow their Twitter accounts and Pinterest boards and purchase their products.

And speaking of twitter, Topsy is a free tool that lets you look up your competitors' tweets all the way back to 2006. Marketing Grade is a free tool that gives each of your competitors an overall score, based on such metrics as social media activity, SEO, and lead generation. And Monitor Backlinks is an amazing keyword tool that enables you to follow the backlinks of your competitors and even have them sent straight to your inbox.

Additionally, you can always type "how to ethically spy on your competition online" into Google for a virtually endless list of competition monitoring research tools and tactics.

CHAPTER 10. CONCLUSION

As you can see, the internet provides a number of completely exceptional ways to research your content.

Sure, you can also use traditional methods like reading books, but these online methods will help you find out what truly matters to your target audience.

Now that you know how to research the best content ideas and what your market wants, it's time to get out there and start creating content. That is what will make you a *true* authority in your niche!

APPENDIX A: RESOURCES

General Research:

Yahoo Answers - http://answers.yahoo.com/

Amazon.com Book Search - http://www.amazon.com/b/ref=usbk_surl_boo ks/?node=283155

http://www.ask.com

FACTS & FIGURES:

U.S. Census Bureau - http://www.census.gov/

MedlinePlus - http://www.nlm.nih.gov/medlineplus/

U.K. National Statistics - http://www.statistics.gov.uk/hub/index.html

Australian Bureau of Statistics - http://abs.gov.au/

Nielsen - http://us.nielsen.com/

Questia - http://www.questia.com/

FactCheck.org - http://www.factcheck.org/

Keywords:

Google Keyword Planner - https://adwords.google.com/

Bing Keyword Research - http://www.bing.com/toolbox/keywords

Wordtracker - http://www.wordtracker.com/

Wordstream - http://www.wordstream.com/keywords

Ubersuggest - http://ubersuggest.org/

SEO Book - http://tools.seobook.com/keyword-tools/

Current Events:

Google Alerts - http://www.google.com/alerts

Google Trends - http://www.google.com/trends/

Social Media:

Facebook Fan Page - https://www.facebook.com/pages/create/

Facebook Graph Search Guide -
https://www.facebook.com/about/graphsearch

Pinterest - http://www.pinterest.com/

Twitter Search - https://twitter.com/search-home

Fiverr (for outsourcing social media account
creation): http://www.fiverr.com/

Organization:

Evernote - https://evernote.com/evernote/

Workflowy - https://workflowy.com/

Scrivener -
http://literatureandlatte.com/scrivener.php

Instapaper - http://www.instapaper.com/

Watching Competitors:

Topsy - http://topsy.com/

Marketing Grader -
https://marketing.grader.com/

Monitor Backlinks -
https://monitorbacklinks.com/

APPENDIX B: TEN TYPES OF ONLINE CONTENT

1) REPORTS & EBOOKS

Your readers might love your blog posts, but everyone seems to have a blog these days. This is why you should release a special report every now and then. Releasing a report or an eBook can help show your audience that you know your stuff and are ardent on providing value.

Reports can be around 7 to 15 pages long. You can either sell them or given them away for free. This can help to build your mailing list or it can be a way to show your customers that you really care.

If you want to save time, you can combine a number of related blog posts into one short report. Reports are simply a more organized way to deliver the information to your readers.

In time, you can even create a longer eBook to sell to your customers as an additional revenue source. Having several free and paid reports and eBooks on your site helps reinforce your position as an expert in your niche.

2) VIDEOS

A video is a great way to deliver content that needs to have a visual element. These can be viewed on YouTube or any other video platform. You don't even need to create new videos. You can take an old blog post or content to create a video and offer your content in a new way.

Video content can be used in all niches, particularly if you want to show people "how to" do something in a more "hands on" way. And showing your face on video can also help to connect people with you on a level that plain text content never will.

3) CASE STUDIES

Case studies can be distributed as a report or they could also make up an in-depth blog posts (with or without video). This kind of content is a way to show your audience how others have been helped from your advice. This can show people who have succeeded using the advice you recommended.

Many times, your customers and readers will create the content for you in exchange for the publicity you give them by sharing it with your audience.

You can also have case studies of you using certain information to help promote products as an affiliate. Nothing promotes trust as well as a well-written case study.

4) INFOGRAPHICS & IMAGES

Infographics can offer highly visual representations of information gleaned from research. They could be an excellent way to display normally tedious numbers and stats in a visual way with good-looking graphics and few words. And statistics show that people love to share infographics via social media.

Let's not stop there though. You want to make sure you are using some sort of image in any piece of content you may share. Images help break up long chunks of text. Images are also far more likely to be shared around social media sites.

5) PRESENTATIONS / WEBINARS

Utilizing a program such as PowerPoint or Slideshare.com, you can bring quality presentations via your blog. This can give your readers a new way to learn things in a visual way, along with the text. You can even have sound on the slides.

This information does not need to be brand new, either. It is only a new way to show what you may have already written. This is good for readers who like to learn in a more "step by step" fashion.

Another idea is to do live webinars. Here, you give a presentation that people can watch while logged into the presentation software on the internet. Google Hangouts is a simple and economical way to run webinars. They can also be recorded for future use too.

6) PRODUCT REVIEWS

Another good way to add other content to your blog is to post reviews on products that you have purchased or received as a gift. In almost every niche there are certain products or services that can help make things easier for you. As an example, if you show people how to grow roses, then you can review your favorite gardening tools.

If you make it a habit to only do review on items you have really used, and are completely honest, you will do well with reviews.

NOTE: if you sell your own products, you can also publish customer reviews people have sent you!

7) CURATED CONTENT

Content curation is all about discovering the most important content for your readers that you can find across the internet. You can then deliver it from one place for your readers through a series of posts describing the content and then giving the link to the original content.

This is a win-win form of content creation. Your audience will like being able to find all the content they need about a given topic in one place. You will be perceived as more of an authority figure in your niche. And this will also save you time when it comes to creating new content.

8) TUTORIALS

Many niches can take advantage of step by step tutorials. Take something you do on a regular basis and turn into an easy step by step tutorial for your audience. An example could be how to upload a video to YouTube on how to prune your outdoor roses.

The value of a tutorial is that your audience will know that you really want to help them be successful. If you are coaching them on how to succeed with the products they buy from you, it will also increase the chances that they will return and buy from you again in future.

You can create tutorials in a number of formats. You can record them as a video or write them out as a document that people can download from your website or read in a blog post.

In time, a good library of tutorials could bring you in a nice bit of search engine traffic.

9) SOCIAL MEDIA POSTS

Remember that posting on social media also counts as content. There are businesses and brands that get most of their customers from social media alone.

Think carefully about the kind of content you post to social media. It should be more about your fans than it is about you. As an example, instead of relentlessly blasting them with links to buy your products, share useful tips and links you think they will like. Sales will follow if you can be of real benefit to your fans.

But don't overdo it by trying to be active on too many social media sites at one time.

10) EMAILS

Last, but not least, remember that every email that you send to your readers and customers is an important piece of content. Email is perhaps more important than any other kind of content you can create.

Once a prospect has signed up to your mailing list, they are giving you permission to contact them directly. You want to keep them happy so that they will always open every email you send to them.

This is why it is also important that you think very hard about content you are going to be sending to your mailing list. Don't just be promoting your products. Send them links to useful blog posts that you have come across, or tips that you have not given to the general public.

Your email list is one of your greatest assets. Treat your subscribers right and your business is sure to profit.

BONUS TIP: RECYCLED CONTENT

One subject you might have observed throughout this guide is that you can reuse and recycle content you already have. That is correct, you can turn old blog posts into new reports, videos, presentations and more.

What makes this work? The fact is that everyone absorbs information in different ways. While some people might prefer to follow your blog and read every post, others might prefer to watch a tutorial in video form, or download an eBook that they can read on their tablet at their leisure.

Recycling your content will not only save you time, it will also ensure that more people get to see your content.

ABOUT THE AUTHOR

My name is C.S. Zahn. I have been an Internet marketer for about 5 years. It's amazing the number of changes I have seen taking place. I am involved in a network marketing company and I am an author on Amazon Kindle. I use a number of different sources when I am writing my books or doing a posting. The things I use most are Google, Yahoo Answers and Facebook. I use the Google Keywords for things like getting ideas for a book title or to see what some of the most popular keywords are in a particular niche. And with Yahoo Answers, this is a great tool to get ideas about what your potential market wants to know about your niche. You can use one particular questions and write an article on it, or you can gather a bunch of questions together and make them headings for chapters in your book. And I have a number of fan pages on Facebook. Here is my author fan page: https://www.facebook.com/cszbestsellingauthor/.

New things are being added every day to help make our jobs as writers, marketers, coaches easier. If you come across a new program that you think would be beneficial, or if it's just not listed here in this book and you think I should look at it, please feel free to send the information to me at cindyzahn@gmail.com or use my Facebook fan page listed above. If I feel that it is worthwhile, I will add it when I do a revision of this book. I will also give you a free plug in the book.